A BRIEF HISTORY OF THE SALEM WITCH TRIALS

Witchcraft Hysteria and Justice in 17th Century Massachusetts

---

SCOTT MATTHEWS

Copyright © 2023 Scott Matthews

All rights reserved. No part of this publication may be reproduced, distributed or transmitted in any form or by any means, including photocopying, recording, or other electronic or mechanical methods, without the prior written permission of the publisher, except in the case of brief quotations embodied in critical reviews and certain other non-commercial uses permitted by copyright law.

Trademarked names appear throughout this book. Rather than use a trademark symbol with every occurrence of a trademarked name, names are used in an editorial fashion, with no intention of infringement of the respective owner's trademark. The information in this book is distributed on an "as is" basis, without warranty. Although every precaution has been taken in the preparation of this work, neither the author nor the publisher shall have any liability to any person or entity with respect to any loss or damage caused or alleged to be caused directly or indirectly by the information contained in this book.

The more that you read, the more things you will know. The more you learn, the more places you'll go. - Dr. Seuss

Contents

Introduction	ix
1. PRECEDING THE TRIALS	1
Early Witch Trials	1
Salem and Salem Village	8
Samuel Parris	11
The Initial Events	15
2. THE FLAME ALIGHT	19
The Accusations Begin	19
The First Three	21
The Examinations and Fates of the Three Women	26
3. THE SECOND WAVE	31
Accusations	31
A List of All Accused	38
4. THE VERDICTS AND THE END OF AN ERA	41
The Survivors	41
The Executed	46
The Names of the Governing	49
The Trials End	51
The Aftermath	53
5. REASONS BEHIND THE WITCH HUNT	57
Medical Theories	57
Puritan Values	61
Misogyny	63
Parris and Politics	66

6. MODERN RECOLLECTIONS 69
  In History 69
  In Memory 72
  In Art 74
  In Culture 77

Conclusion 80

Introduction

Imagine a time when neighborly fights and tense moments with family could lead to execution. This was the harsh reality of the individuals living in Salem Village, Massachusetts, from February 1692 to May 1693.

The Salem Witch Trials were a series of events that led to the deaths of twenty different people. Neighbors turned against neighbors. Family turned against family.

What began as a children's game became a battle of religion, politics, and gossip. Several young girls began to claim that village women were appearing to them as apparitions (ghostly figures) and harming them. Slowly, the accusations piled upon each other as more girls began to claim affliction. The townspeople sometimes reacted with contempt. Sometimes they reacted with outrage. Individuals were punished for defending their families or doubting the claims of the accusers.

Luckily, people in power realized the evils that were taking place right underneath their noses. They began to seek out the end of the trials. Despite this, the history of the trials is so full of sadness and violence that it has permanently impacted the atmosphere of Salem, Massachusetts.

Preceding the Trials

Early Witch Trials

While the Salem Witch Trials are among the most popular instances of witch trials, they were far from the first. Several countries in Europe had already had their share of witch trials beforehand. In addition, some other colonial communities had also already experienced witch trials, although none quite reached the scale of violence of the events that happened in Salem Village.

The first instances of laws against witchcraft can be traced to ancient Egypt and ancient Babylon. In the code of *Hammurabi* (the first legal code of ancient history), witchcraft was explicitly outlawed. While there were no giant witch trials in these societies, individuals were occasionally prosecuted under these laws on a smaller scale.

Similarly, in ancient Greece and Rome, harmful magic was outlawed. Witchcraft and sorcery in general were not considered a bad thing, but magic that could harm others was explicitly banned. They sometimes referred to this as bad medicine or improper medical practice. However, despite the modern name, this usually consisted of people being poisoned by potions or being hurt by folk healing practices. In addition, the ancient Romans specifically outlawed the cult of Bacchus (the Roman god of wine), because of claims that their behavior was immoral. Individuals found to be a part of this group were believed to participate in witchcraft that the Roman society deemed to be of no moral value such as rituals of sex and drunkenness. When caught, members of the cult were executed. These executions only stopped when Christianity was introduced to Rome.

In Europe, a piece of writing known as *Lex Cornelia de sicariis et veneficiis* was responsible for the outlawing of occult practices. After its publication, the prosecution of witchcraft in Rome became more common. Augustus Caesar (the founder of the Roman Empire who reigned as the first Roman emperor from 27 BC until he died in AD 14) attempted to burn any books on the occult that were uncovered in public libraries. Meanwhile, Tiberius Claudius, the second Roman emperor, executed over one hundred people on suspicion of witchcraft.

In the early Middle Ages, witchcraft was still frowned upon but was treated rather lightly. The church at the time believed that the best way to reach individuals engaging in these practices was to treat them kindly and guide them toward the church. The leader of the church at the time declared it to be a serious crime to burn witches, and anyone caught doing so would be executed.

In general, the church maintained this view throughout the Middle Ages aside from a few theologians (religious scholars) who specifically held deep-seated resentment for pagan (non-Christian) practices. Most theologians claimed that there was no reason to burn witches because witches simply did not exist. They believed that it was a false practice and ultimately it would be a greater evil to execute people for it than to ignore it. Unfortunately, this did not stop individuals and communities from executing those they believed were witches.

During the time of the Inquisition (a period when the Catholic church went to war against those who spoke against God), some individuals who were deemed witches were executed by the church. However, this only happened in instances where these supposed witches engaged in heresy, an action where one speaks directly in opposition to church beliefs. The Pope, the leader of the church, declared that only when heresy was involved could execution take place.

The declaration of Pope Innocent VIII marked a startling change in doctrine. He declared war against devil worshipers and encouraged Christians to find and punish them. He issued a Papal bull, a type of public decree issued by a pope of the Catholic Church, in 1484, declaring witches as evil and dangerous. Three years later, the witch-hunting manual *Malleus Maleficarum* was written.

The *Malleus Maleficarum* (Latin for "The Hammer of Witches") is a treatise written in 1486 by Heinrich Kramer, a German Catholic clergyman. The book was later endorsed by the Catholic Church and played a significant role during the period of the witch hunts in Europe.

The *Malleus Maleficarum* is essentially a guide for the identification, prosecution, and dispatching of witches, according to the beliefs and methods of the time. It details the forms of witchcraft and methods of combating them, and it underscores the existence of witches as a real and potent threat to Christendom.

The work is divided into three sections. The first asserts the reality of witchcraft and refutes those who deny it. The second outlines the forms of witchcraft and the remedies against them. The third part is a guide for judges on the procedures for discovering and convicting witches.

It should be noted that, while the *Malleus Maleficarum* played a considerable role in the witch trials of the 16th and 17th centuries, it is largely discredited today as a result of significant shifts in scientific understanding and religious and social attitudes. Today, it is studied primarily as a historical artifact, demonstrating the superstitions and fears that pervaded society in the late medieval and early modern periods.

After the publication of this manual, actual witch hunts became common in Europe. There are too many to name, but the greatest number of people were tried and executed during the Thirty Years' War (from 1618 to 1648), one of the longest and most dangerous wars in European history. During this period, the church declared witches to engage in cannibalism (the eating of human flesh), infanticide (the killing of babies), and immoral sexual practices. Several countries partook in large witch hunts, including England, Denmark, and Scotland. During this time, using special tests to determine if one was a witch was the most common way of trial.

These early tests included throwing individuals into the water to see if they would sink or float, as well as pricking their skin with a needle to see if they would bleed.

When the Puritans of England moved to America to establish colonies, they took their fear of witches with them. The first set of witch trials in the colonies took place in Springfield, Massachusetts, about forty years before the events of the Salem Witch Trials.

Salem and Salem Village

The little dwelling of Salem Village was excited to finally break free from the control of the larger city of Salem. Formerly known as Salem Farms, the village had finally been permitted to form its own fully functioning church. In the past, the individuals living in the village were forced to travel to the main town each sabbath (a day of religious observance and abstinence from work) to attend church. This church was known as the First Church of Salem, and although the service was wonderful, the journey there could be challenging as families were forced to cross several miles of land.

Several other villages had already been granted the right to form their municipal governments and found their own churches. The villagers of Salem Farms longed to do the same. The transition began in 1672 when the village was designated as a parish, a local church community with its own priest, but it was not yet classified as a town. This allowed the villagers to build a church and appoint a minister, but it did not offer the wide range of benefits that other towns had been given. Salem still collected taxes from the inhabitants of the village and now they were faced with an additional tax intended to go to their chosen minister.

The ministers chosen to lead the church in Salem Village had to be unordained, which means they weren't officially authorized as ministers. The government of Salem feared that allowing a fully ordained minister to run the village church would give more power to the tiny dwelling. Thus, the ministers could not baptize anybody or hold communion. If one wished to participate in these sacraments, one had to travel to the main church in the larger city.

The church in the village became a heated talking point for the next few decades. Ministers were loved by some but hated by most. Multiple individuals held the position, only to be removed by force when they upset the congregation.

Eventually, this led to a man named Samuel Parris being named the minister of Salem Village.

Samuel Parris

Samuel Parris was born to a family that openly rejected the Church of England. His family lived comfortably but was not considered rich by any means. Finding no reason to remain in England, Samuel moved to Boston, Massachusetts, as a young man. He attended Harvard College, then he temporarily moved to Barbados to run the sugar plantation he inherited from his father. This plantation was eventually ravaged by a hurricane, leading Parris to sell his land in Barbados to return to Massachusetts, bringing his slave, Tituba, with him.

After returning to Boston, he fell in love with Elizabeth Eldridge and they quickly wed. Three children were produced from their marriage: Thomas, Elizabeth, and Susannah. Eventually, Samuel decided to join the ministry to secure financial stability for his family after his ventures as a salesman proved fruitless. He was already a member of Boston's First Church, which was headed by Reverend John Oxenbridge, his uncle. He became an affiliate preacher, an individual who is able to preach but is not a full minister, to the church in 1688, and he was stationed in the settlement of Stow for some time.

During his time in Stow, Samuel was confronted by elders from Salem Village. They wanted him to become the preacher at their church. Parris was perplexed by their request. He knew many men with more qualifications than him who were seeking ministry work at the time. He had not even graduated from Harvard, while these other men had graduated and also had years of experience in the clergy.

It's believed that the elders likely chose Parris for his relation to Boston's First Church. Many Puritans were fighting against the liberalization of the church during this period. Several churches had adopted the Halfway Covenant, which allowed individuals to receive baptism without stating their conversion experience, a process where members would explain why they wanted to enter fully into the church. In addition, these members were able to baptize their children despite not being full church members. The First Church was against this doctrine, which appealed to the elders of Salem Village.

Samuel Parris was then ordained (made a priest). The three magistrates of Salem village attended the ceremony. Reverend Nicholas Noyes, who was the assistant minister of the church in Salem, conducted the ordination. Also in attendance was Reverend John Hale, a minister from Beverly, and Reverend Samuel Phillips, a minister from Rowley. At this point, the little church in Salem Village was now able to operate as a fully functioning church.

Parris was a sacramentalist. He believed that baptism and communion were the most necessary parts of church attendance. He founded his new ministry based on the idea that these sacraments should form the foundation of the church. His sermons focused heavily on this theme and he preached the importance of full baptism—an open rejection of the Halfway Covenant. He openly mocked the villagers for not fully participating in church life, and he claimed that their actions had angered God. He painted himself as the savior of their problems, asserting that his ministry would make God pleased with the village once more.

Initially, church membership grew. People were committing to full membership, despite the influence of churches following the Halfway Covenant. However, the congregation stopped growing after a year or so. Parris began preaching against those who refused to attend the church. He saw them as "others" to be fought against. Yet, Parris did not realize the effect of his intolerance until late in the year 1691, when the villagers refused to pay their taxes so that Parris could be paid his salary. Parris responded by declaring Satan to be the cause of the villagers' actions. Thus, it comes as no surprise that Parris found Satan's presence in his own home.

The Initial Events

In February of 1692, two young girls in the minister's own home began to display odd behavior that frightened those closest to them. His niece, Abigail Williams, and his daughter, Elizabeth "Betty" Parris, both began experiencing episodes of bizarre speech and poor behavior, which were immediately deemed spiritually suspicious by the militant pastor. Samuel Parris quickly brought together a council of religious men to review the situation. This council consisted of magistrates (judges) from Salem, as well as some nearby ministers. This included Reverend John Hale, John Hawthorne,

Bartholomew Gedney, Jonathan Corwin, and Reverend Nicholas Noyes.

The men determined that the events taking place were of supernatural origin. Lucky for the girls, the men decided that somebody had bewitched them, making them innocent despite their actions. Had the girls been deemed possessed by demonic forces, they would have been blamed for their own bizarre behavior. The treatment for the bewitchment consisted of prayer, readings from the scripture, and fasting. This was the most common treatment for bewitchment at the time, as many Puritans believed that God would eventually deliver them from evil if they had faith in him.

Initially, Samuel Parris adhered to this concept. He called in a local doctor for a second opinion, only to be told once again that the cause was supernatural. Parris continued to wait for weeks until he finally grew tired of watching the children's behavior worsen. He called in another doctor hoping to find an answer. This doctor was a fellow associate of Boston's First Church named William Griggs. Griggs confirmed that the initial diagnosis was correct.

Soon after the diagnosis by Griggs, more girls fell ill. Ann Putnam, the twelve-year-old daughter of Thomas Putnam, and seventeen-year-old

Elizabeth Hubbard, niece of Dr. William Griggs, both began behaving oddly. At this point, the magistrates of Salem grew extremely interested in the situation. They began to look towards the book *A Memorable Providence* by Cotton Mathers, a man known for his experience in witch hunting, in order to gain insight into the situation and develop a course of action. Meanwhile, Parris doubled down in claiming that Salem Village was overrun by evil.

His sermons blamed the villagers for the bewitchment of the children. The accusations took on a more active tone shortly before the children began to speak of witches. Parris claimed that "assistants of Satan" could be found in Salem Village, indicating that individuals were actively worshiping or working with the devil in the little Puritan town.

The Flame Alight

The Accusations Begin

In late February of 1692, a woman named Mary Sibley made the mistake of requesting a "witch cake" be crafted. This special cake was to be made of a mix of rye meal and the urine of the afflicted children. It was then meant to be fed to a dog and tossed into a fire. Supposedly, this was intended to give the afflicted children the ability to name the individuals who bewitched them. John Indian and Tituba, Parris' slave, were the ones who made the cake.

While Parris declared the cake to be diabolical and evil, the girls were able to name who they believed bewitched them afterward. Mary Sibley apologized for her poor judgment in asking for the cake to be made. Luckily for Mary Sibley, the congregation forgave her and she managed to avoid becoming a victim of the Salem Witch Trials. Unfortunately, the creation of the cake was the catalyst for the hunt to begin.

The afflicted children became a public display. Instead of continuing with the prescribed procedures of fasting, prayer, and Bible readings, Parris exposed the public to details about the bizarre behaviors of the young women. His daughter was spared from the debacle, as she had been sent to live with a relative in Salem. However, the other children were encouraged by the congregation. They were asked to name the individuals responsible for their afflictions and, on February 29, they alleged that Sarah Good, Sarah Osborne, and Tituba, Parris' slave, were accountable for their bewitchment.

The First Three

Sarah Good was an impoverished woman. While her father was a financially successful tavern owner, Sarah did not receive an inheritance upon his death, as the small amount allotted to her was taken by her mother's new husband.

She had no skills, no land, and no money for a dowry. She settled into a struggling marriage with an indentured servant (a person who had to pay off their debt via acting as a servant) named Daniel Poole, and after his death, married a weaver named William Good.

Sarah and William lived in poverty. Their survival depended on the kindness of the inhabitants of Salem Village. They went from house to house, begging for scraps of food or small amounts of money. Yet, the townspeople found Sarah to be rather unpleasant even when they were exceptionally generous. She often left their houses mumbling to herself and rarely seemed happy. In addition, Sarah did not attend church. Her excuse was that she did not have proper clothing to wear to the service.

When Abigail Williams and Betty Parris accused her of witchcraft, the villagers immediately believed it. Suddenly, Sarah's discontent mumbles were now spells intending to inflict harm upon those who showed her charity. They claimed that Sarah wanted to inflict pain on the town due to jealousy. Good denied the accusations.

Sarah Osborne, on the other hand, was once a very wealthy wife of a man named Robert Prince. Prince was brother-in-law to John Putnam, a member of the wealthy Putnam family. The couple had three children—Joseph, James, and Elizabeth—before Robert died. After Robert's death, Sarah hired an indentured servant—an Irish immigrant named Alexander Osborne.

She fell in love with him and they wed after he paid off his debts. However, Sarah made a decision upon the wedding that greatly upset the traditional town of Salem Village. Instead of leaving her husband's property to their sons upon his death, she kept them for herself and Alexander. This led to legal battles between Osborne, her children, and the Putnam Family. In addition, Osborne had not attended church in three years due to symptoms of what we now know as depression.

Thus, it comes as no surprise that Sarah Osborne was among the three women blamed for the affliction of Betty Parris and Abigail Williams. Elizabeth Hubbard also accused Sarah Osborne of being her tormentor. The girls described the events as Osborne poking them with needles. Osborne denied the allegations.

The final woman accused of witchcraft was Tituba, Samuel Parris' slave.

Tituba was Native American and had lived in Barbados as a slave for some time before traveling with Parris to Salem Village. She was married to John Indian, another Native American. It is believed that Tituba was exposed to witchcraft and folk magic during her time in Barbados, leading her to tell the children stories containing supernatural elements.

These stories ended up causing her downfall. Betty and Abigail asserted that Tituba was the third individual responsible for bewitching them.

Tituba initially denied these claims, then eventually, she confessed to making a witch cake, speaking to the devil, and learning about the occult from her mistress in Barbados. These confessions gave the villagers a cause to further investigate each woman.

The Examinations and Fates of the Three Women

The cases of Sarah Good, Sarah Osborne, and Tituba began on March 7, 1692, after a warrant had been issued to arrest the three women a week prior. The women were examined in court in order to determine the court's course of action. Sarah Good and Sarah Osborne declared their innocence. Tituba, on the other hand, pleaded guilty.

During Sarah Good's trial, the children who accused her began to behave bizarrely in the courtroom. At one point, one child had a seizure. The child asserted that she had been attacked and produced a portion of a knife. Luckily, a young man was able to claim the broken weapon and explain that the child had likely stolen it. The judge gave a mild admonishment to the young woman but overall seemed to believe that Sarah was still guilty. Despite this, Sarah Good maintained her innocence.

Tituba was asked to give her account of the situation. Tituba admitted to devil worship but claimed that Good and Osborne were truly to blame. She stated that Satan, who was dressed in all black, had asked them all to sign his special book. Tituba declared that she had initially said no, but then she continued to state that Good and Osborne forced her to sign her name anyway. She mentioned that there were six additional names in the book, but that dark forces had rendered them unreadable to her. She stated that there were as many as nine other witches in Salem, all of whom sought to harm the children of Samuel Parris, the children of Thomas Putnam, and the relatives of William Griggs.

She stated that Sarah Good also specifically attacked Elizabeth Hubbard by commanding her cat to scratch the girl. She claimed that Good also had control over a variety of wild birds that she could send to bother the young girls. Tituba then said that she could see that Good was holding a yellow bird, and despite the obvious empty hand of the woman, the accusers agreed.

Word of Tituba's examination was spread far in the Puritan world. Even churches far away were scared they might be in danger too. Meanwhile, her words were examined and twisted in every possible way by Samuel Parris and the magistrate. It is now believed that Samuel Parris coerced Tituba's confession by beating her the day before. Court records indicate that she had a lot of bruising on her body on the day of her examination.

Tituba's examination led Good to declare her innocence. She also claimed that Tituba and Sarah Osborne were witches to seem more credible to the court. Meanwhile, Sarah Osborne also maintained that she was innocent, but she did not accuse anybody else of witchcraft. Tituba, ironically, also declared her innocence. She stated that while she did participate in the activities mentioned, it was done under coercion. She stated that Good and Osborne threatened her life. She had to participate or else they would remove her head. The women were all then taken to jail to await an official trial.

Before Sarah Osborne could face trial, she died in jail. This happened on May 29, 1962, after years of fighting an unknown illness. It is believed that the conditions of the jail expedited her death.

Sarah Good gave birth during her time in jail. The child passed away shortly after. Good was eventually allowed to stand trial. Twelve jurors found her guilty despite her testimony and she was sentenced to death. On July 29, 1692, Sarah Good was hung.

Tituba continued to make bizarre statements throughout the Salem Witch Trials. She spoke of unholy creatures with both human and animal body parts. She told stories of witches controlling cats, wolves, and rats. She was held in a jail known as the Boston Gaol for over a year. Samuel Parris refused to pay the necessary fines to free her. She was eventually sold to somebody who paid her fees. The buyer's identity remains unknown.

The Second Wave

Accusations

Shortly after the arrests of Sarah Good, Sarah Osborne, and Tituba, more children asserted to be afflicted by witchcraft. Ann Putnam Jr., Mercy Lewis, Mary Wallcott, and Mary Warren were among these children. Ann was a friend of the first three girls to claim affliction and would eventually accuse over fifty individuals of witchcraft. Mercy Lewis was an orphan who worked as a servant in the Putnam household. She was extremely close to Ann. Mary Wallcott was Ann's closest friend aside from Mercy. Mary Warren, on the other hand, was a servant for the Proctor family.

Not long afterward, the girls began to directly accuse individuals of practicing witchcraft. Martha Corey was an outspoken critic of the witch trials. She believed the accusing children to be lying and claimed the villagers were all paranoid. Ann Putnam, to silence her, proclaimed her to be a witch on March 12, 1692.

Seven days later, Abigail Williams made another accusation. Rebecca Nurse, a seventy-one-year-old woman known for her devotion to the church and community, was declared to be a witch. The village initially reacted in shock and outrage. A petition was passed around declaring her to be innocent, which even her enemies agreed to sign. The examiners, John Hawthorne and Jonathan Corwin, exhibited empathy during her examination. Nurse did not waver in her faith during this period, fully believing God would allow her to go free due to her innocence.

On March 26, another supposed witch was revealed. Only four years old, Dorcas Good was accused of witchcraft by Mary Walcott and Ann Putnam Jr. Dorcas was the child of Sarah Good, leading to her being viewed as potentially more dangerous than one would assume. Walcott and

Putnam claimed she attacked them like a wild animal, biting and scratching them. Dorcas, being only four, quickly admitted to witchcraft when pressed for information and agreed that she had witnessed her mother speaking to the devil.

Two days later, Elizabeth Proctor was accused by Mercy Lewis of being a witch. Mercy asserted that a ghostly form of Proctor was haunting her. This happened shortly after her husband, John Proctor, had ignored Mary Warren's claims that Giles Corey, the husband of Martha Corey, was similarly appearing to her. Their dismissal of her claims likely caused the girls to become upset and set the Proctor family as their next target.

Initially, the community was doubtful of the claims made against Elizabeth Proctor. Mercy fell into a mock trance and attempted to act as if she was being tormented by the woman. When the villagers did not believe her, she stopped and immediately stated that she was simply joking. However, three days later, both Mercy Lewis and Abigail Williams once again asserted that Elizabeth Proctor was a witch. They stated Elizabeth was finding ways to cause them stomach upset and make them feel as if she was pinching them. They also stated that now they were seeing the ghostly form of John Proctor. Once again, the townsfolk started a petition to declare that the Proctors were great citizens and likely innocent.

Shortly after, another near-identical petition was compiled.

On April 3, Sarah Cloyce became the next victim of the witch hunt. Sarah was the sister of Rebecca Nurse, and since Nurse had been accused, she vehemently declared her sister to be innocent. This happened shortly after a Sunday service where Sarah walked out early. Samuel Parris had read John 6:70, "Have I not chosen you twelve, and one is a devil." This led Sarah to leave as a protest to her sister's situation. It was shortly after this that Abigail Williams and Mary Walcott began to claim that Cloyce was also a witch. John Indian, a servant of Samuel Parris, also accused Cloyce of witchcraft. It is also around this time that Mary Warren admitted that she had lied about the witches, stating that the other girls involved had also lied.

Ten days later, Ann Putnam Jr. made another accusation. She claimed that Giles Corey, the husband of Martha who had been accused a month prior, was spiritually attacking her. Giles was shocked, as he had been a part of the group of villagers who wanted to fight the supposed witches. He had believed the accusations against his wife to be true. Knowing that he was innocent made him reconsider the entire situation.

On April 19, another woman was accused of witchcraft. John Putnam and a man named Ezekiel Cheevers reported Bridget Bishop on behalf of several young girls: Ann Putnam, Mercy Lewis, Abigail Williams, Mary Walcot, and Elis Hubert. Once again, the girls claimed that a ghostly apparition of the accused was physically attacking them. In addition, Ann Putnam stated that Bishop openly referred to Satan as her chosen God.

Some adults also began accusing Bishop of harming them. One couple, Richard Coman and his wife, asserted that Bishop regularly attacked them in bed. Another woman claimed that Bishop managed to tear her clothing. William Stacy, a townsperson, also stated that Bishop openly worshiped the devil and Bishop's husband claimed the same. Another townsperson, Samuel Shattuck claimed that Bishop had harmed his child with a spade. He also stated that Bishop had him help her dye pieces of lace used for poppet making. Poppets were small dolls used for witchcraft. Other townsfolk asserted to have seen Bishop with a collection of poppets in her home.

Around this time, Mary Warren had been accused of witchcraft by Ann Putnam and Abigail Williams. She immediately took back her statements about the accusations they had made. She said that the accusations against the villagers were true. She stated that she had claimed otherwise out of fear. The townspeople believed her and she was able to join her friends on the accusing side once more.

On April 22, Mary Eastey was accused of witchcraft as well. She was the sister of Rebecca Nurse and Sarah Cloyce. Mercy Lewis claimed that the ghostly apparition of Mary Eastey had assaulted her in her sleep. Eastey declared her innocence and defended herself with grace. She stated that she had never worked with Satan but had instead spent her life fighting against him.

The oddest accusation, however, came on May 4. George Burroughs, a devout Puritan and former pastor, was accused of witchcraft. He was not accused by the group of girls that had accused most of the other villagers. Instead, people from his former church had accused him due to hostility surrounding unpaid debts. Despite these deaths in relation to the accusers being known, the accusations were still taken seriously.

A List of All Accused

Several more individuals were also accused, although their impact on history is not as great as those mentioned beforehand. In order to show the number of people impacted by the witch hunt, the surnames of the accused are listed below in alphabetical order:

- Daniel Andrew
- John Alden, Jr.
- William Barker, Sr.
- Mary Bradbury
- Bridget Bishop
- Reverend George Burroughs
- Martha Carrier
- Giles Corey
- Martha Corey
- Lydia Dustin
- Mary Eastey
- Philip English
- Mary English

- Edward Farrington
- Martha Farrington
- Abigail Faulkner, Sr.
- Ann Foster
- Dorcas Good
- Sarah Good
- Dorcas Hoar
- Elizabeth Howe
- George Jacobs, Sr.
- Susannah Martin
- Sarah Morey
- Sarah Osborne
- Alice Parker
- Mary Parker
- Sarah Pease
- Elizabeth Proctor
- John Proctor
- Ann Pudeater
- Wilmot Redd
- Margaret Scott

- Ephraim Stevens
- Roger Toothaker
- Tituba
- Samuel Wardwell, Sr.
- Sarah Wildes
- John Willard

The Verdicts and The End of an Era

The Survivors

Believe it or not, a good number of individuals survived after being accused of witchcraft. While few of them were declared not guilty, many managed to survive due to extenuating circumstances or eventually being pardoned while awaiting execution.

The following individuals were the only four that were found not guilty after standing trial: John

Alden Jr., Ephraim Stevens, Mary Bradbury, and William Barker Sr. While not much information is available on why Ephraim Stevens was released, there is an abundance of information on the vertex of the other three.

John Alden Jr. was declared not guilty because he had fled and hid upon hearing of being accused. He waited to come out of hiding, not doing so until the end of the Salem Witch Trials. Shortly after coming out of hiding, he was proclaimed innocent.

Mary Bradbury was initially found guilty. She had been sentenced to execution, but her friends continued to petition to delay her execution. They were successful in their attempts, leading her to still be alive at the end of the trials. She was then proclaimed innocent and released.

William Barker Sr., on the other hand, was believed to not be innocent at all. While he denied participating in witchcraft, he also cooperated with the courts and the accusers. He begged for forgiveness and expressed sorrow despite being innocent. He also gave information on other accused individuals. This led to him being acquitted and released despite the jury believing him to have committed acts of witchcraft.

One person, Elizabeth Proctor, managed to avoid execution with the help of luck in time. Proctor was found to be pregnant at the time of her sentencing. While she was sentenced to death, the court required her to be kept alive until the child was born. By the time the child was born, the events of the Salem Witch Trials were over. This led to the release of Elizabeth Proctor instead of the state executing her as initially planned.

Three individuals fled as soon as they heard they were accused. Unlike John Alden Jr., they never were openly acquitted after they fled. These people include Daniel Andrews, Mary English, and Philip English. Andrews never returned to Salem. Meanwhile, Mary and Philip temporarily relocated to New York but eventually returned to Salem long after the events of the witch trials were over.

Two individuals were released on bond rather than imprisoned or executed. They were deemed to be of low risk to the community, and both were later acquitted after the trials ended. These two people were Dorcas Good and Sarah Morey.

Several other individuals were found guilty but pardoned. Abigail Faulkner Sr. was pardoned due to pregnancy. Dorcas Hoar confessed and was pardoned for being willing to do so. Sarah Pease was pardoned at the end of the trials with many others who had been accused, but not tried.

Edward and Martha Farrington were also pardoned for reasons that have not been recorded.

Tituba was also eventually pardoned. Although she had been imprisoned after admitting to witchcraft, she was rewarded with a pardon for being helpful to those investigating. She was then sold to an individual who also paid her jail fees.

Sarah Cloyce also managed to avoid execution. This is because although she was accused and examined, she was never actually indicted. Unfortunately for her, both of her sisters were indicted.

This is not a complete list of the individuals who were accused and survived. History has lost many names to time. In addition, the hysteria spread to other towns, leading to additional victims who were either exonerated or executed. These individuals are not mentioned in this book because technically they are not part of the Salem Witch Trials.

The Executed

The following individuals were executed after being found guilty of witchcraft: Bridget Bishop, Sarah Good, Rebecca Nurse, Elizabeth Howe, Susannah Martin, Sarah Wildes, Reverend George Burroughs, George Jacobs Sr., Martha Carrier, John Proctor, John Willard, Martha Corey, Mary Eastey, Mary Parker, Alice Parker, Ann Pudeater, Wilmot Redd, Margaret Scott, and Samuel Wardwell Jr.

These people were executed primarily by hanging. These hangings often took place in front of crowds of spectators. Multiple individuals were hung at one time. Often, the spectators consisted of both adults and children. Relatives of those being executed also attended in sadness and mourning as they watched their own families be executed.

One individual, Giles Corey, was executed in a different way. Corey had refused to confess despite pressure from the jurors and the magistrate. He was repeatedly encouraged to confess despite him already being found guilty and sentenced to execution. The belief was that by confessing, he would potentially have the ability to save his soul. When Corey refused, he was executed by being forced to lie down with a board on top of him. Rocks were slowly piled up on the board, suffocating him. The intention was to hopefully force him to confess. It is unknown if they would have stopped the execution had he confessed. Despite the painful torture he endured, he maintained his innocence as he slowly suffocated to death under the weight of the rocks and boulders placed upon him.

Ann Foster and Sarah Osborne both died in prison. Both were likely to be executed had they survived, but they died shortly after being in prison due to already being in poor health. Another woman, Lydia Dustin, had been acquitted. She still died in jail, however. She was to be kept in jail until her fees were paid. She did not survive to see that happen. Finally, one individual died in prison before his trial. Roger Toothaker was treated poorly in jail while awaiting trial and died before his court date.

The Names of the Governing

The following individuals were magistrates during the Salem Witch Trials. While historical records and literature on the trials primarily give information about the victims, these people played an important role in the events and should be remembered for what they did. The magistrates were: William Stoughton, John Richards, Nathanial Saltonstall, Waitstill Winthrop, Bartholomew Gedney, Samuel Sewall, John Hawthorne, Jonathan Corwin, and Peter Sergeant.

The clergy (religious leaders) involved in the trials were as follows: John Hale, Cotton Mather, Increase Mather, Nicholas Noyes, Samuel Parris, Samuel Willard, and Thomas Barnard.

These individuals were responsible for spreading the hysteria that caused the trials. In addition, they played key roles in the court proceedings, as well as in the sentencing and execution of many innocent people.

The Trials End

Shortly after many of the executions, the governor of the province at the time grew concerned about the use of spectral evidence (the claim that spirits were visiting a person) in the trials. This governor, William Phips, believed that spectral evidence relied too much on the idea of people being truthful. In addition, in Puritan society, it was known that the devil could take the shape of other individuals. Under the Puritan belief system, it was possible that one's spirit could appear to somebody, but could actually be the devil in disguise. This means that some of the people who were being accused were potentially innocent even if the afflicted children were telling the truth about the apparitions.

Upon further investigation, the governor also realized that a large number of faithful and moral citizens had been tried and executed during these trials. On October 29, 1692, he officially suspended the trials and released everybody in prison on bond. Cotton Mather, a key figure in the history of witch hunts, openly expressed distaste for this decision. He acknowledged that some innocent people may have been executed during this time, but he stated that God would never allow the devil to appear in a human form without their consent.

His son, Increase Mather, directly declared that he believed the opposite. He spoke of the book of Job in the Bible. He stated that one cannot assume that God will prevent suffering or prevent the devil from acting on an individual.

In January 1693, the trials began again. However, the usage of spectral evidence was no longer permitted, resulting in the suspension of a significant number of trials once again. Soon after, the governor pardoned everyone involved and ended the witch trials.

The Aftermath

The colony formally apologized after the trials ended. People were declared innocent that initially were found guilty—whether they were still alive or already dead. The individuals involved were compensated for their suffering. If they were dead, their families received the money. This did not come until the year 1700, however. The individuals involved and their families had to plead with the courts for some form of restitution (justice). By the time they received it, many of them had already suffered greatly in loss.

Most of the judges and public figures involved in the trials issued halfhearted apologies, most of them blaming the trickery of the devil for why they participated in the trials. Samuel Sewall took partial responsibility, asking God to forgive him.

Betty Parris, Ann Putnam Jr., Abigail Williams, and the other girls who were the main accusers also blamed the devil for tricking them. Nobody blamed the girls for the evils they committed. Ann Putnam Jr. was the only one who ever openly admitted her mistake. Despite the evils the girls committed, they all grew up to have relatively normal families and lead average lives.

Samuel Parris still attempted to remain in town as the minister of Salem Village Church. He too blamed the devil for his role in the trials. Suddenly, his preaching about evil and witchcraft changed into preaching about the power of love and forgiveness. However, he was not forgiven. Individuals who had previously tried to run him out of town used the events of the witch trials to get rid of him. They claim that he pressured the court to accept spectral evidence, something that was not typically considered acceptable during trials.

Parris tried to apologize again, this time for believing in spectral evidence. Yet, he still attempted to hold onto his power in the village.

In 1697, he was forced to resign by a council of ministers. He was replaced by Joseph Green, a minister who made it his mission to help the community heal from the evils they had endured.

Green preached about forgiveness and encouraged neighbors to forgive one another for the events that took place. He reversed decisions of excommunication that had been made during the trials. He reassured the community that none of their executed loved ones were in hell, an idea that had been spread by Samuel Parris.

Some of the individuals involved were not sorry for their role and held firm that the people executed were guilty. John Hale, for example, wrote *A Modest Inquiry*, a book explaining his beliefs about how the individuals executed were all truly witches. He doubled down on these claims, stating that he believed that the witch hunts should still be ongoing, as witches were likely still in Salem Village.

Luckily, the Enlightenment began shortly after the end of the trials. Puritan beliefs began to slowly fade out and wither away. Accusations of witchcraft became rare, and actual trials related to the accusations became even rarer. While some of the Puritans attempted to hang on tightly to their beliefs, the religion had essentially died out by the 1800s.

Reasons Behind the Witch Hunt

While there's no definite proof behind any of the theories mentioned in the next chapter, they all have evidence that makes them plausible. Scholars believe that it is likely not a single theory that is correct, but rather a combination of many or all of them. Truly, we will never fully know why the Salem Witch Trials took place.

Medical Theories

Scientists have spent large periods of time dedicated to studying the potential medical reasons behind the behaviors of the accusing girls. The girls suffered from bizarre behaviors, epileptic-like fits, and claimed to have experienced things that were simply not possible. Whether these behaviors were due to a medical problem or a psychological problem, it is generally accepted that the true issue lay within the accusers and not within the women they claimed to be witches.

One major theory behind the accusations made is that they were caused by hysteria. Often, individuals with delusional beliefs related to fear would spread their fears to others in the community. Psychologists claim that it is possible that one of the girls genuinely believed that she was being attacked by a witch. By talking to her friends and the other girls in the community, the idea of witchcraft was spread. This could have spread fear and led to the community seeing witchcraft where none was present. Similar attacks of hysteria were found in colonial communities regarding issues such as attacks by Native Americans and the spread of illness.

Another theory behind the events of the Salem Witch Trials is that the accusers were potentially experiencing the effects of a potent psychedelic poison. Convulsive ergotism was an illness caused by ingesting a type of fungus that often grew on rye bread. This fungus, Claviceps purpurea, can cause hallucinations and psychedelic experiences. This is the type of fungus that LSD is often derived from and the effects are very similar.

Some scientists suggest that it is possible that the girls were infected with a form of encephalitis, an inflammation of the brain, that was carried by birds. Lethargic encephalitis sometimes results in bizarre behavior, periods of deep sleep, and hallucinations. If the girls were exposed to the virus from wild birds, they could have developed encephalitis that led to their behavior and later accusations.

Another key explanation involves sleep paralysis, a natural event when a person's body stays asleep as their minds awaken. Individuals who experience sleep paralysis often also have terrifying, vivid hallucinations. Sleep paralysis would make a lot of sense in the context of the experiences of the accusers as they stated that most of the witches visited them as an apparition as they were trying to sleep in bed at night. This would also explain the attacks and the difficulty of fighting off the apparitions as one can experience uncomfortable sensations and are usually unable to move.

Of course, there are endless other possibilities. Epileptic seizures could be the cause of some of the fits that the girls experienced. In addition, febrile seizures, or fever-induced seizures, are also a large possibility. If the girls first fell ill, had seizures, and then received attention due to them, the accusations may have been an attempt to keep that attention going long after their illness was over. There are many other disorders of the brain and nervous system that have the potential to have caused the symptoms the accusers displayed.

Puritan Values

The values and beliefs of the Puritans contributed heavily to the atmosphere and background of the witch trials. Puritans believed that mankind was naturally wicked. Christ's salvation was deemed the only way for one to make it into heaven. In addition, to be a moral person, individuals were believed to have to fight their natural impulses. This belief alone made it easy to believe that the villagers accused were willing to commit crimes against their fellow neighbors.

The Puritans also believed that God knew who was going to heaven before they were even born.

They believed that he would only send the Holy Spirit to those that he had selected and that the Holy Spirit would guide them to righteousness. Those that were not selected by God would be damned to hell.

There were several church laws that the Puritans held dear. Breaking the laws would upset the leaders of the church and had the potential to bring an individual under intense scrutiny from the congregation. Missing church was considered a violation of Puritan law. As mentioned previously, missing church was often used as evidence of one being a witch. In addition, people were expected to work hard and conform to society. This led to individuals like Sarrah Good, who were seen as lazy or outcasts, being labeled as witches.

Misogyny

Misogyny, or the belief that women are inferior to men, also played a large role in the events of the Salem Witch Trials. Puritan beliefs considered women to be weaker-willed than men. It was known in the Puritan community that individuals of weaker will, such as women and children, were at risk of being tempted by the devil. It was stated that the devil did his handiwork through the weak minds of these people.

In addition, in several witch-hunting manuals that were used during this time, women and femininity were classified as inherently evil. These books stated that women were prone to seeking out the devil and were often unsatisfied with living moral lives. The witch-hunting manual *Malleus Maleficarum*, written by Johann Spregner and Heinrich Kraemer, states that existing witches recruit new witches by first causing misfortune in the lives of other women. Then, they introduced the victims to the concept of witchcraft and devil worship as a means to end their suffering and solve their problems.

The willingness of women to participate in these activities was blamed on their having weaker physical bodies and a tendency to gossip. In addition, women were declared to be emotionally unstable, which supposedly made them more likely to practice witchcraft during moments of anger or sorrow. Women were also considered to be less intelligent than men, a trait that supposedly made them easy for devils to trick.

Many Puritan scholars also believed that some of the witchcraft-related behaviors that had to be done by sorcerers included sexual activity with the devil. Thus, this alone made women more likely to pursue witchcraft, as the devil was a male figure. Of course, some men were still accused of witchcraft, but this was significantly rarer.

Due to all of these beliefs about women and the nature of witchcraft, women were seen as natural scapegoats when witches were suspected. It is unknown why Puritans were so inclined to view women in such a harsh manner, but modern feminist scholars suggest that these views impacted the fate of those accused of witchcraft. It was primarily women who were executed during the trials, all of whom were innocent.

Parris and Politics

It is believed that Samuel Parris may have taken advantage of the accusations in order to secure his spot as minister of the Church of Salem Village. The villagers had begun to refuse to pay their taxes and generally were not fond of Parris around the time that the young women claimed to be afflicted.

The young women initially did not begin by directly accusing anybody. Instead, they simply began to act in odd ways. It is possible that Parris may have exaggerated their behavior or encouraged their behavior in order to draw attention to them. Once the girls began discussing witchcraft, Parris saw an opportunity to rally the villagers around him. He painted himself as a protector of the village, a warrior fighting Satan.

By spreading the hysteria that the village was under attack, he increased the villagers' attendance at church and made them feel as if they needed to support him in such a dangerous time. In addition, many villages feared that if they expressed discontent towards Parris at that point, they could potentially be the next accused. This is especially likely due to Parris' relations to some of the accusers.

In addition, other individuals related to the accusers seemed to use the hysteria against their enemies. The Putnam family used Ann's role in the witch hunt to punish those who had wronged them in the past. It is likely that the families of the other girls involved may have also played a similar role.

Modern Recollections

In History

Historically, the Salem Witch Trials are looked back upon with horror and sadness. Many innocents who were of devout Christian faith were accused of unspeakable deeds and acts of witchcraft. When individuals speak of burning witches at the stake, they are actually referring to women whose only crime was catching the attention of vengeful young women.

The first to note the evils of the Salem Witch Trials were a group of religious people known as the Quakers, a religious group that held values conflicting with Puritan beliefs. About three years after the events of the Salem Witch Trials, the Quakers openly declared the entire witch hunt to be a tragedy. They prayed for the victims and held fast days in their memories.

Shortly after the Quakers openly declared their sorrow, people who were involved in the trials began expressing remorse for their actions. One individual, Thomas Fiske, brought together eleven other jurors to express remorse and sorrow for their actions. In 1703, the new Reverend of Salem Village Church undid the excommunication of Martha Corey. Three years later, in 1706, Ann Putnam Jr. asked for forgiveness for her role in the trials. Ann was one of the most vicious accusers, targeting more individuals than any other girl; she declared that it was she who was tricked by Satan. She stated that the devil had tricked her into accusing innocent souls of witchcraft, which led to their deaths. According to church records, she was forgiven for her actions and was welcomed into the congregation.

Several people who had been accused but were not executed were able to petition the government to reverse their ruling. Those who sent petitions were granted exoneration. In 1709, a petition was sent to the government listing twenty-two individuals who deserved exoneration or to be declared innocent. This petition was initially denied, however, the decision was reversed two years later by the governor of Massachusetts. In addition to being exonerated, people named in the petition were also compensated for their suffering. Those who were executed had their portion of the compensation given to their living relatives and descendants.

As time has gone on, the families and descendants of the accused have sought out justice for those who were executed for these supposed crimes. Although some individuals had been pardoned shortly after their executions, many were not exonerated until years later. It was not until November 2001 that the state of Massachusetts officially declared all of those who had been harmed and found guilty during the witch trials to be innocent.

In Memory

Several victims of the Salem Witch Trials have had special memorials erected in their honor. In addition, there have been many memorial events for the victims of the witch hunt, many of which still take place today.

On the Nurse homestead, a large memorial was erected in honor of Rebecca Nurse. Her descendants put up the memorial as a reminder of the evils done against her and as a reminder of the pious (devoutly religious) woman that she was. The initial memorial was erected in 1885 and, in 1892, an additional memorial showing appreciation to the neighbors who signed a petition in favor of the exoneration of Rebecca Nurse was added to the plot of land.

In 1992, a park in Salem, Massachusetts, was officially dedicated to the victims of the Salem Witch Trials. In the park, stone benches were included for each individual executed during the trials. The nearby town of Danvers also erected a memorial for the victims.

In 2017, a team of researchers found the actual site where the executions took place. A nearby place used for spectating was also discovered. The spectator area was named Proctor's Ledge. The city turned this specific area into a special memorial referred to as Proctor's Ledge Memorial.

In Art

The Salem Witch Trials have influenced a variety of literature and media. The story has been used repeatedly not only to scare people but to teach the dangers of letting fear control them. Additionally, numerous authors have utilized this narrative to illustrate the perils of alienating and discriminating against one's neighbors.

Young Goodman Brown was a tale written by Nathaniel Hawthorne, published in 1835, that used the idea of a town of witches. In the story, Goodman Brown meets with the devil in the woods, thinking that the meeting is a secret. Slowly, they make their way to the center of the forest only to find the entire village is there participating in a ceremony of witchcraft. Brown sees his wife there and is heartbroken, having previously believed her to be a woman of faith. Suddenly, he wakes, uncertain if the events were real or a dream. The moral of the story is to avoid immoral temptations, as one may discover more than one wants to.

H.P. Lovecraft (American 20th-century writer of weird, science, fantasy, and horror fiction) used the trials to create his own setting of Arkham, Massachusetts. According to Lovecraft, Arkham was founded by individuals who had fled from Salem during the time of the witch hunt. This place was a setting for several of his stories and, while he never officially wrote about the Salem Witch Trials, the history of the trials obviously influenced the stories set in Arkham.

The Salem Witch Trials are also very popular in Hollywood. Movies such as the *Lords of Salem*, *The Covenant*, and *The Autopsy of Jane Doe* capitalize on the fear the tales induce. Secretly revealing the main antagonist of a horror film to have been a witch during the time of the Salem Witch Trials has become a trope in Hollywood. Meanwhile, television shows involving witches such as *The Chilling Adventures of Sabrina* and *Charmed* often make references to the witchhunt via comments and character names. Other television shows, such as *American Horror Story* and *Vampire Diaries*, have used the trials as a background for certain characters.

The most popular piece of media surrounding the Salem Witch Trials is *The Crucible*. *The Crucible* is a play written by Arthur Miller that uses the backdrop of the Salem Witch Trials as a metaphor for McCarthyism, a practice in 1950s America that consisted of people being encouraged to report potential socialists and communists. Miller's play has since been adapted into an opera, as well as into several movies. The play focuses primarily on the home of John Proctor. In the story, John is having an affair with Abigail Williams. This is what leads to the events of the witch trials. While the story is not historically accurate, it still reflects the horrors and lessons of the actual witch trials.

In Culture

The Salem Witch Trials were a horrific historical event. It turned Salem into a city of sensation for modern pagans and for horror enthusiasts. Every Halloween season, Salem, Massachusetts, is flooded with tourists looking to enjoy a witchy atmosphere. While the city hosts a bunch of witchy events during this time, they primarily focus on sharing the message about the dangers of accusing individuals wrongfully. Despite this, people say that vacationing there during the fall months can be extremely fun and a great family experience.

One of the main attractions is the Salem Witch Museum. The first part of the museum consists of a reenactment of the trials by various statues with pre-recorded audio. Afterward, individuals are invited to hear stories of the trials and to discuss the horrors behind the event. Finally, the moral lesson of the dangers of letting fear control you is emphasized. The museum is primarily meant to show people that the scariest part of the trials were not the supposed witches, but the very human mistakes made that harmed innocent people.

The city also hosts a walking tour. This tour takes tourists to the historical sites where the most important events of the witch trials happened. Many people assume that the tour is meant to be spooky. However, the city makes it clear that it is not a ghost tour or a scary tour. Instead, it is purely historical and meant to educate individuals about the events that happened in 1692.

There is also a ghost tour of the city. However, this tour is not as promoted by the city as many of the more historical attractions. In general, the city tries to avoid exploiting the dead that were already exploited so long ago. Of course, several entrepreneurs have taken advantage of the spooky history and atmosphere behind Salem. These individuals have opened up witch shops and horror-themed restaurants in various attractions that are meant to have a spooky atmosphere. Whether or not these attractions are appropriate given the history of the town, they are unfortunately very popular amongst tourists.

Hollywood has also capitalized on the history of Salem. While the movie *Hocus Pocus* is not about the events of the Salem Witch Trials, its creators chose to include the trials in the main character's backstories. Several attractions in the city revolve around the *Hocus Pocus* movie, furthering the town's affiliation with witchcraft.

Conclusion

The Salem Witch Trials were an extremely dark period of pre-American history. The hysteria caused by the young group of girls killed many individuals and negatively impacted an entire community. Samuel Parris was also responsible for these evils. Whether it was due to his eagerness to rope the town into joining his congregation or due to a true fear of the devil, he let his religious convictions lead him to have several people killed.

The trials showed many flaws in the Puritan colony's justice system. Just three years later, people began to admit that the events were a giant mistake in a true tragedy. Women and men were painted as agents of Satan due to barely believable accusations made by young girls who were still technically children. These individuals were forced to have a trial with no lawyer. Often, accusations of the girls were deemed to be more reputable than the explanations of the accused. No individuals were safe. Some of the most religious and pious people were among those executed for witchcraft.

While today the victims of the trials are properly honored and memorialized, many people still mourn for the innocent lives lost. Meanwhile, the media continues to use the history of the witch trials as inspiration for a variety of media—some of which are exploitative. However, the story of the trials does act as a great metaphor for the dangers of fear and separating oneself from other community members.

Salem, Massachusetts, is now a city known for Halloween and witches. While the city attempts to be respectful to the victims of the witch trials and share their knowledge of the evils that happened during this time period, entrepreneurs in the area are fighting to make it a spooky vacation spot.

Overall, the world will never forget the events of the Salem Witch Trials. However, it is unknown whether or not the world has truly learned from the horrors that have happened. Hopefully, we will continue to discuss the topic and properly memorialize the victims involved.

Bonus!

Thanks for supporting me and purchasing this book! I'd like to send you some freebies. They include:

- The digital version of *500 World War I & II Facts*

- The digital version of *101 Idioms and Phrases*

- The audiobook for my best seller *1144 Random Facts*

Scan the QR code below, enter your email and I'll send you all the files. Happy reading!

Find more of me on Amazon!

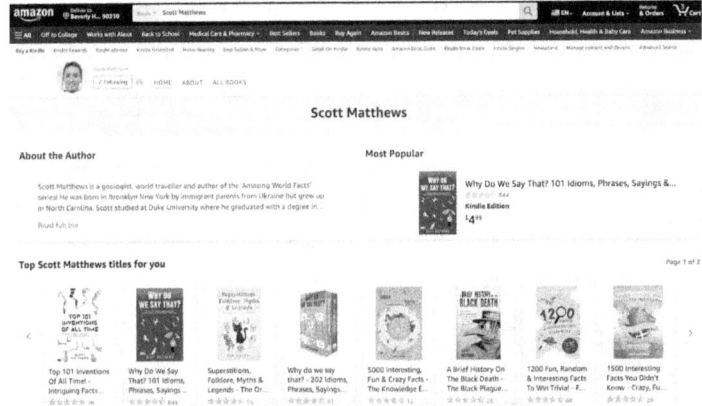

Check out the "Amazing Facts" series and learn more about the world around us!

Check out the "Why Do We Say That" series and learn where everyday idioms and phrases come from!

www.ingramcontent.com/pod-product-compliance
Lightning Source LLC
Chambersburg PA
CBHW072103110526
44590CB00018B/3296